Small Words

insatiable

JUDY KENDALL

CinnamonPress

INDEPENDENT INNOVATIVE INTERNATIONAL

2520cu llanl

Published by Cinnamon Press
Meirion House,
Glan yr afon,
Tanygrisiau,
Blaenau Ffestiniog,
Gwynedd, LL41 3SU
www.cinnamonpress.com
The right of Judy Kendall to be identified as author of this work has been
asserted by her in accordance with the Copyright, Designs and Patent Act,
1988. Copyright © 2015 Judy Kendal
ISBN: 978-1-909077-71-3
British Library Cataloguing in Publication Data. A CIP record for this book
can be obtained from the British Library.
Designed and typeset in Palatino by Cinnamon Press
Original cover design by Jan Fortune-from an image by Judy Kendall.
Printed in Poland
Cinnamon Press is represented in the UK by Inpress Ltd
www.inpressbooks.co.uk and in Wales by the Welsh Books Council
www.cllc.org.uk

Acknowledgements

The many gardeners who have inspired me at the Incredible Farm, Incredible Edible Town Garden Group and Ferney Lee Gardening Group; Incredible Edible Todmorden's Mary Clear and Estelle Brown for getting me to write vegetable haiku; Venerable Amaranatho for gardening-inspired wisdom; Tim Carey for everything, first at Oakcroft Gardens and then with Frank Bowman at the wonderfully-named Welhealth Incredible Edible Gift Economy Agroforestry Eco Farm, Tyn Y Nant; Bridget Kendall; Ursula and Kate Hurley for a residential digging workshop; Salford University for a sabbatical in which to garden; Sue Bartlett and Malc Binstead for a Malvern writing space; and, of course, the brilliant Jan Fortune and the team at Cinnamon Press, especially Adam Craig for his collaborative, creative typesetting.

'My Northern Flowerbed' was runner up in the International Cinnamon Press Poetry competition; a number of the vegetable and fruit haiku feature on Incredible Edible Todmorden's edible poetry site
www.incredible-edible-todmorden.co.uk/blogs/?c=edible-poetry
and on banners around Todmorden, illustrated by Estelle Brown.

Contents

for Tim Carey
a gardening inspiration
good at growing much more than nettles

insatiable carrot

allelopathy

shears have a spot of rust a drip of snow from when I last delved in the garden chest melting snowdrift piles by back door print spots of cat fox badger follow retrospect pads sudden deeper imprint muscles flex and push the body up jump the fence collecting firewood a long dead branch uncovered down under the laburnum tree ALL PARTS POISONOUS SEEDS PETALS FLOWER-BUDS LEAVES BARK ROOTS NAUSEA VOMITING SLEEPINESS CONVULSIONS COMA FROTHING AT THE MOUTH UNEQUALLY DILATED PUPILS better not burn that fill the trug dry lifeless soil with reddened fir under which no SUN NO NUTRIENTS PINE NEEDLE ACID ALLELOCHEMICALS NOTHING GROWS twigs from the heap in the garden to dry under which slugs growl grass yellows

Anxieties and Influence

it rains so much it must
be good I thought to dig
a bed and then it snowed
, so much I couldnt sow
the plants I bought

snow i
s good
it brea
ks up t
he soil
and ad
ds moi
s t u r e

**people think snow and ice are g
ood breaking up the soil but if y
ou dig a bed before the winter a
nd it has all winter and then the
snow as well it is too much**

I dont need moisture it rai
ns all the time
but I only dug mine tw
o weeks ago

when i
t melts

silence

was that not enough?

My northern flowerbed

shovelling snow
off the unseeded flowerbed
hard, iced up, cold
through polyester trouser-legs
through wellington soles
through doubled woollen socks
too cold to plant or sow
the way the snow lies now
deeply by the outer gate
shoved up towards
the front end of the bed
more than the back
striped with patterned sun
almost warmed
scattering heat degrees
the rocky poor-soiled yard
with hardly any left
to fall, so thinly spread, upon the bank
my frozen northern bed

Done with gardening

after ten minutes
I am done with gardening

press on

bite-sized goals:
one trugful of leaves
  two trugfuls
    when the composter's full
      after I've swept the steps
        retrimmed the xmas tree
          laid fire to use up pine needles
            shifted wood
              collected up the rubbish

                mite-sized hauls:
                  rubberbandpricetagredplasticbrokencarmirrordustbinlids
                    metrelongstripofplastic
                      emptycokecan, not mine, rolling over to next door
                    splitbagofconcrete
              scrunchedpaper
        rolledbamboomat, soaked in week-old rainwater caught
      muddied at the bottom of one bin

Preparations
West Yorkshire, March 2013

I

   three jerseys   coat fur hat
climb up from the yard
   thick scarf   fingerless gloves
duck under the barbed wire
     plastic mug of rooibus
spilling at the bark and growl
   next door neighbour's dog
her rush forward in mock charge
it's mine   scared   indignant
body held tight down   ears flattened
commotion   *gerrout*   teeth bared

   striding past
     ms cerberus
       well-beaten
       wet paths
     to where
      trees round
     someone brought
     a sleeping bag
    in the last snows
     so he had two he said
      and wasn't cold
   secluded flat views

               lovely spot

     downwind
large animal   not dog
   flash   white behind
Another   following
    head-on
   full doe-face   doe-ears

II

clipping the old brown Xmas tree
  faint wet cedar smell
    lift shake twirl
with snipped twigs –
  pine needles sinking to gravel

        move the tree to *oh wow 2 blue tits*
             on the laburnum   have to get that birdbox up
  the flagstones and get the trug.

    all in the planning.

  takes sixty minutes to cut hair well.
kindling fills the trug in ten
  shears   dried and oiled in twelve

      hairdresser to a shaven tree
        no style or shape but take care
      to gather up the end-product
          what falls upon the floor   lies there
      attracts attention far far more
        than thinning trimming bushy hair

ownership

untouchedbybrokerclaims
ownershipofthedogsoderi
lictbrokenupclaimingown
ershipofhowpathclaimsow
nershipofthebramblesclam
Imownershipofallthegrassc
lameownershipoftheretoday
claimsownashipofthepathly
lanehandownershitofthedo
gainedohnotshithaofthebra
mblyodoursheofthegrassed
seedupnobrokerwillltouchit

ignorance of weeds

weeding ignorance
nettles   grass
the only things I recognise
all green to me

dandelions showering
early nettle, young tender leaves
I weed in spurts
pre-flowering

foragers leave to harvest
traditional horticulturalists pull up
    eat them   bin them

what of edibility?

        can I be sure this huge crop I'm hauling in
is dandelion
        all dandelion?
   should I pull only plants I don't?
  trug of nettles, dandies, grass
  neglected sweepings from the front steps / path

holes I make from pulled dandelions
    holes I need for divided bulbs

  wellies   knife   fork   gloves   bag
 in   porch   ready for   next

     gardening

                    let it spread   head-
        on   proceed
                          pick one

  as method   lay it down

                      like weeds

     like dandelion

moving from empty: particle study

indoors too long because of snow too long decapitated when planting out too long too strong too long indoors too long because of snow too long decapitated when planting out too long too strong too long indoors too long because of snow too long decapitated when planting out too long too strong too long indoors too long because of snow too long decapitated when planting out too long too strong too long indoors too long because of snow too long decapitated when planting out too long too strong too long indoors too long because of snow too long decapitated when planting out too long too strong too long indoors too long because of snow too long decapitated when planting out too long too strong too long indoors too long decapitated when planting out too long too strong too long indoors too long because of snow too long decapitated when planting out too long too strong too long **indoors too long because of snow** too long decapitated when planting out too long too strong **too long** indoors too long because of snow too long decapitated **when planting out** too long too strong **too long** indoors too long because of snow too long decapitated when planting out too long too **strong** too long indoors too long because of snow too long decapitated when planting out too long **too strong** too long too **long indoors** too long because of snow too long decapitated when planting out too long too strong too long indoors too long because of snow too long decapitated when planting out too long too strong too long indoors too long because of snow too long decapitated when planting out too long too strong too long indoors too long because of snow too long decapitated when planting out too long too strong too long indoors too long because of snow too long decapitated when planting out too long too strong too long indoors too long too strong too long toostro ng too long

18

plant me a slice of beans, says Jack

from weeding to hoeing to planting in rows to searching for sticks to string
up the string reeds bend on haunches where oaks will twisting left fall or s
tanding break stooping right spade from weeding to hoeing to planting in ro
ws from weeding to hoeing to planting in rows to to searching for sticks
to string up the string reeds bend on haunches where oaks will twisting left
fall or standing break stooping right spade inside out cant dig in zig zag sn
ap wiggles from weeding to hoeing to planting in roreeds bendarching for s
ticks to string up the strion haunches bend on haunches where owhere oaks
will left fall or standing break stooping right twisting left inside out cant di
g fallig zag snap wiggles from weeding to hoeing to planting in rowor stand
ing searching for sticks to string up the string reeds breakn haunches wher
e oaks wilstooping right falspade inside out cant digooping right spade insid
e out cant dig in zig zag snap wigglin zig zag weeding to hoeing to planting
in rows to searching for stick snaptring up the string reewiggles on haunc
hes where oaks will twisting left fall or standing break stooping right spad
e inside out cant dig in zig zag snap wiggles from weeding to hoeing to plan
ting in rows to searching

five or so at a time

Fairy tales shorts

Jack Be: UP FIVE DOWN

Sle Be: PRICK DOWN KISS UP

Sn W & 7 D: MIRROR OUT APPLE DOWN KISS UP

Cinder E: OUT PUMPKIN IN

Lit Rd Hd: TO FOREST IN STOMACH

P Piper: LIMP BEHIND LEFT

be quick to catch the runner bean

Detective gardening

separating herbs from uninvited comers
teasing out plants, nettles even, caringly

parsley — flat / curly-leafed, at sides in full weed
basil — medicinal, in clumps everywhere weedless

delicate soft job, replanting herbs
consider ratios — mass : volume : weight : mobility

> the more feathery seeds wash off the camber of the bed
> olfaction of plant consequent detraction rate thereof:

> citronellol | linalool | myrcene |
> pinene | ocimene | terpineol |
> linalyl acetate | fenchyl acetate |
> trans-ocimene | 1.8-cineole |
> camphor octanane | methyl
> eugenol | methyl chavicol |
> eugenol | beta-caryophyllene

V
erge

peeling the turf
easier than scab-picking

break &
    virginal territory
        enter

garden | house divide

civilization –
as thin as that?

indoor clogs wet soil

welly-earth kitchen

mudprint hall

Garden rhythm

the hard graft:
no topped peaks, no bagged mountains, no buzz

sowing, weeding
tomatoes, fruit-trees, spinach

sun, nutrients, water, time
agents of patience when conditions benign

seeds form shoots form buds form fruit

but in this spring of snow
the seed that was sidesteps the season
vegetable love turns sloth
stays seed, leaves off, abandons growth

art of shearing grass

it doesn't take long
though grass grows
six inches in two
 weeks in may it
doesnt take long
shearing uphill is
 easier you can see
the strands you
havent sheared
dandelions distract
 sheared grass is
great for horses if
you forget to oil the
shears grass tipped
 over barbed wire
into the horses' field
will hang on the
wire cut grass can
 be gathered up in
 hands a rake is
better wait for the
 grass to stand up
again and shear
once more not trim
as a lawn but
quickly looks better
than it was can bear
 being untidy for
longer a little
meadow at the side
of the house a little
patch for dandelions
yes sprightly nettles
 yes the
occasional

blu
ebe
ll

Finally sun

2nd day running at least
       no excuse
              though I find one

at the top of the bank
all frost melted off

the gooseberry bush bare not dead-looking
the tayberry bit of green

the transplanted holly, dry, stick-like
by the path a vibrant shoot —
not the best place for prickles

sliced fungi lie in the wet grasses
like logs with spongy middles

near the brambles
the already blooming blueberry
an immobile raspberry twig
positions determined by contours and daffodils

              neighbours see me
                     embedded on the bank
                     footholds above them
                            but not each other

              they answer to
                     'a lovely day'
                     'won't keep you'
                            neither realise we are a group of three —

       what the dogless neighbour makes of
              'Tilly's not growling at me now'
                            god knows

A little hedge-cutting?

trying to clip the roadside hedge
I decide backwardly on tools
fetch out the shears
veer to the tug
and after, unmethodically
add the stepladder
broom, gloves...

or would an electric trimmer
have been better?

cutting vertically
arms stretched wobbling
to the pinnacle hedge-
clippings tumble
to jacket pocket
stick in eyes, ears,
body wedged
on woodwormed ladder
treads seesaw
computing, tricky, head

the shears are safer

tall green mild and meek
not quite the full onion
the gentle leek

Insatiable appetite for poetry

I am trying to write out
a carrot poem on a carrot
poem in permanent marker
pen <oh mad potter> on a
carrot that keeps getting
absorbed into carrot
<what insatiable
appetite it has
for poetry>
processes
indelible
inedible
carrot
poem
not t
o be
fed
to
h
o
r
s
e
s
!
as
poem
carrot
process
for poetry
appetite it has
<what insatiable
absorbed into carrot
a carrot keeps getting
write <mad potter> on
the poem I am trying to
on carrot poem on carrot

Insatiable appetite for poetry

Crow look out

I am not habitual
sun-rise sun-high-in-sky
   eyelids lift
   memories thud
come-go

   directly I put seed out
on the hilltop porch
   swoop form roof to sycamore
poise for my exit back indoors
   personless moment

   down on the railway bridge I
lurking shifts
   shit-black dashes   the trees, the sky
perched on   surface
  bowl of cloud
     crow look-out   utmost branch
   crow nest-twigs
can they really see so
  need-sharpened sight
   viewing my house   there
  bird feeder, sun
               seed

thin dark leaves on
hunky trunky clumps of tree

o broccoloccoli!

Chicks

watching chicks *edeitp meec*
*nartchtyhr*How d'you kill them?*ols lim*
this, says K *elauqe* He picks one up and pulls
*spmeecnartc*I'm only showing you *wolslauq edeitp*
nartci if I was going to kill I'd twist its neck*ty lswols*
*rel*The compost smells of donkey poo *wolslauqedeitpm*
eecpeel It is donkey poo *wolsqedeitpml* I know it from two
hours of sho *cnart*planting seeds of common mallow, Chinese
lantern, ballhead onio*artcimhtyh* transplanting curly parsley (slow
to) *olslauqed eitpmertcim* and really red deer tongue*wolslauqedeitpm*
*eecnar*freshly foraged bitter cress curry *rwolslauqe ertcimhtyhrypeel*
little dips of conversation in a calm and spreading pool *ecnartci*
*mhtyhrypeels wo*They're *hcimhtyhr* the ch *wolslauqedeitpl* icks poo in
their water *qed eiimrypeel* D's silent hand removes the container
for refill *ht yhr yaude* squabble with it*mecnl*Some chicks intelligent,
says C*w,ol sl imheel* Not these, I reply *elswolsla* They're still young.
Tmhtyh rypeelswolslauqedeitpmeecnartypeel N and I could watch them
all day *ewols llauqe*They nearly fly — spread wings beautiful *tyhry*
wolsla uqedeitpmeecnartcimhl One is smaller, whiter head *empti empti*
cimhtyhrypee lswcna How can people eat chicken *wolslauqedeitpm*
*eecna cnartcil*K and X describe their favourite chicken sauce Don't
be so tactless! Right in front of the*cna.*Even the dog is whining
*wdeitpmeer tcim*That's cos he wants to eat them, says K*wolsl* T
photographs the chicks for the blog *sw olsl* packet*c wolslauqe dei*
*tpmeec*to my pulled greens *wolslauqed* The power of advertising
peelswolsl says T *wolslauqedeitp lslauq edei tpm eecnar tcimh peel*I could
watch them forever *eec* says neighbours*e elseel* 3am cock
crow*eitpmeec nartci m t*I offered to kill him and bring them chicken
soup, says K*wry pelswols cnaeel* That bought him 6 months more
life*pti ewolsla uqedeitpme* quite good really*epw olsluqedei tpmeecartci*
*wolslau q edeimeecnmhtyhrypeell*A boy used to go after the eggs but
he's better now … goes fishing *eepyrhy*
thmic tr ancee mptiedequalslowsleepmictran
leepyrhythmictranced e ceemp
trance empti ed equ

Quiet, concentrated

Can you hear the woodpecker over there, quite far?
Once heard not silenced
Very quiet, concentrated

Maj Seedling Plum, Opal Plum
Ogg Plum, Michaelmas Red

Randomly planted beds / tyres

Lemon Pippin, Dennisons Supreme
Ellinson Orange, Johnagold

I get stuck in
Memory holds three trees at once

Irish Peach, English Codling
Damson

Fingers dig wet woodchip / grass
For tree signs

Grampa Buxton, Greengage
Arthur W Barnes

Sitting on tyre edge
Standing in bed

Megans Tree, Winston
Worcester Pearman, Bramley

eat standing
roll round roof of mouth
little steamed pumpkin

K explains grafting *Shakespeare grafting Buckingham.* and I understand for the first *Her royal stock graft with ignoble plants* you can't just grow new apples — *Richard III, act iii, sc.*)apple-pip tocrab-apple, if you're lucky *Dauphin.*it's like you need to cut off your finger *O Dieu vivant! shall a few sprays of us Our scions, put in* To clone another you*wild and savage stock,*grumpy, I make a messy sketch of the newlygrafted trees*Spirt up so suddenly into the clouds,* (twigs) *And overlook their grafters? — Henry V, act iii, sc. 5 (5).*It's the best spot, they tell me *King.* birds, *His plausive words* view, *He scatter'd not in ears, b ut grafted them,*sheltered from the wind*To grow there and to bear.*T says it's a special job — *All's Well that Ends Well, act i, sc. 2 (53).*aren't all jobs special? *Perdita. The fairest flowers o' the season Are our Carnations and streak'd Gillyvors Which some call* **Gardener, for giving me this labelling job of woe,***nat garden's slips of them,* **Pray God**the **plants thou graft'st may** never grow.*P olixenes*Wherefore, gentle maiden, Do *you neglect them*but I do enjoy the robin's *song But Nature make* and the warmth when the sun com*es out Which you say adds to Vines Nature, is an art we*marryand you can't identify a grafted*tree A gentle wildest* stock,for seven*years*A *nobler* race: stanley knife peels plastic off the graft *joins*this is*what did they use before pl*astic does cloth?b*utitself is*nature. *astards. Perdita.*I nick myself, blood kee*he dibble in the earth to set one inter's*metallic iron taste, bandage, accident book*Tale, act iv, sc4 (81)*one of my unpicked grafts *ating plants by grafts,*twig scion toppling off twig stock*cuttings*I try to slot them back*artificial*I'm understanding grafting better *in Shakespeare's day,*rain drops*a see*exactly like t*a d ash* for the polytunnel*hose of our own or*Howsing exhibition of rootstock

Grafting

35

Potting trees I knife fork right size / right colour plant pots flowering
trees splinted cuttoforceoutblossom trees *Egremont Russet, Bloody
Ploughman's, Fiesta* II knife round fork into pot cover roots stand
straight look pretty *Fiesta? Bloody Plough?* III signs / pencil for
unlabelled trees ONLY THE FRUIT WILL TELL REAL SCIENCE IF THEY COME BACK IN
FIVE YEARS AND SAY YOU SOLD ME A FIESTA NOT A PLOUGH I'LL SAY, WELL YOU
GOT FRUIT IV carry two to repository return pull out more pots *dig,
pot, dig, pot* V knife fork right size / right colour plant pots forget slight
resistance flowering all linted cuttoforceoutblossom trees *Egre*ree / soil
in p*mont Russet, Bloody Ploughman's, Fiesta* II knif round fork in*ging
to pot cover roo*pot and straight please pretty Fiesta? Blo *digugh?* III sign
s / pencil for unlabelled trees ONLY THE FRUIT WILL TELL REAL SCIENCE IF THEY COME
soil turn leaf to help escape BACK IN FIVE YE p inside *pot dig, pot, dig, pot*
ARS AND SAY YOU SOLD ME A FIESTA NOT A PLOUGH I'LL SAY, WELL YOU GOT FRUIT IV
pot XII watch dog com carry two to reposito *dig, pot* Potting trees I
k ry return pull out more pots *dig, pot, dig, pot* V alternation of jobs d
c minimise muscle strain forget slight resistance *Blo*rking alone *dig*s,
Fiesta II knife r *dig* VI put right amount of roets soi nd straight look
pretty *Fiesta? Bloody Plough* in pot p ns / pencil for unlabelled trees ONLY
upright *pot, pot* VII enjoy thrush company singing on *dig, pot, dig, pot*
SOL VIII sl *FIESTA* asure getting good *dig, pot, dig, pot* IX worms know two
to reposi squirming *dig, pot* t m *pot X* cut dust sore part with ternation
of jobs minimise m soil turn leaf to hel scape po sistance to working
alone *dig, dig* VI put ti ear up inside pot e *ig, po* il in pot pot full tree
upright *pot, pot* VII enj *t, dig, pot* XI wa hgro singing on *dig, pot, dig,
pot* VIII slight pleasure g wers wander watch *dig, pot* IX worms know
squirming *dig, pot, dig, pot* X stroll wat ore part with soil turn leaf to
help escape pot earth up insid ch gaze a *pot, dig, pot* XI watch growers
wander watch stroll watch g t sheep po ep *pot, dig, pot* XII watch dog
come over sniff *dig, pot, dig, t, dig, pot*g trees I knife fork right size /
right colour plant pots flower XII watch plinted cuttoforceoutblossom
trees *Egremont Russet, Bloody* dog comm*an's, Fiesta* II knife round fork
into pot cover roots stand straigh e look pretty *Fiesta? Bloody Plough?*
III signs / pencil for unlabe over sniff ONLY THE FRUIT WILL TELL REAL
SCIENCE IF THEY COME BACK IN FIVE YEARS AND SAY YOU SOLD ME A FIESTA NOT
A PLOUGH I'LL SAY, WELL YOU GOT F *dig, po* carry two to repository return
pull out more pots *dig, pot, dig, pot* V alternation of jobs minimise
muscle strain forget slight resistance to working alone *dig, dig* VI put
right amount of tree / soil in *dig, pot* t full tree upright *pot, pot* VII
enjoy thrush company singing on *dig, pot, dig, pot* VIII slight pleasure
getting good *dig, pot, dig, pot* IX worms know squirming *dig, pot, dig,
pot* X cut dust sore part with soil turn leaf to help escape pot earth
up inside *pot dig, pot, dig, pot* XI watch growers wander watch stroll
watch gaze at sheep *pot, dig, pot* XII watch dog come over sniff *dig, pot,
dig, pot* Potting trees I knife fork right size / right colour plant pots
flowering trees splinted cuttoforceoutblossom trees *Egremont Russet,
Bloody Ploughman's, Fiesta* II knife round fork into pot cover roots
stand straight look pretty *Fiesta? Bloody Plough?* III signs / pencil for

[I'd have called
those grafted apple trees
twigs]

Pink trug

develop a headache working alone
cleaning donkey-composted soil of plastic in the polytunnel
and sticks that, decomposing, use up nitrogen.

mmmmy nails are black, mmmy thumb-skin rough, mmy clothes/
boots slightly muddy.

lunch talk ricochets from the centre of the earth
to walls around our galaxy, molecules bouncing.

interest but no passion
more headache, tired, begrimed
…… and too much bread ……

is it the first day,
working the soil, cleaning the toxins,
warm under plastic, slow pace

want to dance from task to task rush
achieve complete finish practise brilliance.

Gardening's not like that.
drawn-out simple on-going tacks,

burning face, the walk here lovely
pink trug, bought on the way home

excellent.

hairy bitter cress
going wild
among
the cabbages

risk

putting the birdbox back
trunk to steady
up the bluetits are

for W forget
him or myself
waiting I hold the slight

headache stinging
hands on one side
face numb

a bath a lie down
choc | caffeine lindor easter egg
withdrawal? flu?

to wash to warn
nothing goes in
mouth without

sweeping up every part of the
laburnum tree is pods they
get everypoisonous

where

risk

ootbarkflowerbudleafpodseedrootbarkflowerbud

rootbarkflowerbudleafpodseedroot
barkflowerbudriskootbarkflo
werbudleafpodseedrootbark
flowerbudriskootbarkflowerbud
leafpodseedrootbarkflowe
rbudriskootbarkflowerbudleafpo
dseedrootbarkflowerbudr
iskootbarkflowerbudleafpodseed
rootbarkflowerbudriskoot
barkflowerbudleafpodseedrootb
arkflowerbudriskootbarkflow
erbudleafpodseedrootbarkfl
owerbudriskootbarkflowerbud
leafpodseedrootbarkflowe
rbudriskpodseedrootbark
flowerbudriskootbarkflowerbu
dleafpodseedrootbarkflow
erbudriskpodseedrootba
rkflowerbudriskootbarkflow
erbudleafpodseedrootbarkfl
owerbudriskpodseedroo
tbarkflowerbudriskootbark
flowerbudleafpodseedrootbark
flowerbudriskpodseedro
otbarkflowerbudriskootbark
flowerbudleafpodseedrootbark
flowerbudriskpodseedro
otbarkflowerbudriskootbark
flowerbudleafpodseedrootbark
flowerbudriskpodseedro
otbarkflowerbudriskootbark
flowerbudleafpodseedrootbark
flowerbudrisk

Go[ ]dilock

weeding first my bed
I turn   other kind of animal
invader in possess[ ]er inter fear a
  shrug on animal become
suck chewing mash
 a lips teeth gum
   the various   greens   browns
of animal   on briefly animal
      unknowing the   the
shrug brief   off
  day after
        how
days after
       spar[ ]e how bar[ ]e
  what deeply weeded it is
   who what go[ ]dilocks
an animal I became
  that garde
   a bed   ?

turd

nicking some of nick's real coffee, milk
   caught short on the walk home
a lump of turd in your knickers
no bushy verge to hide it

no people around
so whip a hand down the back of your tracksuit
and bring up the lump
small coal, hot midden

no place to throw it
canal one side: river the other

you could wait till you cross the road and find some grass
but walking past people holding this....

canal   river?
river   canal?

river
        throw it in

below a small rapid
it bobs
and floats
you should have known

 walk further
wipe your hand on soggy moss

That is a first

Compost

so
two loos
pee + non pee
all matter reused
how can we pee in the pee loo
Frank's radio an MDF-thickness away
the already damp forest countryside at our disposal
not to mention the post haste benefits of steaming compost waste?

Rural Idyll

horse flare nostrils flank in out foreleg trembling

leg within
  leg caught   FIELD
two legs without

kicks   kicks
 barbed wire
thrashing to get free
 thorn branches
wire caught
netting

 sound of struggling
young owner
BO BO STOP IT
tumbling
push him back
turn over
white face BO shock black
YOU'LL HURT
YOURSELF hair pretty

two legs within

                                     FIELD

two legs without

Bo nibbles broken branch
flank heaving
barbed wire bout

blue blue

oh what an awful thing
to come and see the blue blue in my face
sky water come
all through the window that I left
how did he open no what can we
leave my do not go the bird looked
scathingly to give
less hope yes ways up water
from beyond   beyond
oh coming yes

oh

blue blue blue

the redder the grape
the better for heartache

best : worst

before I could say

I wish like anyone I never loved

(and that's the best of it)

like this

wish I could say

I never like anyone I loved before

(and that's the worst of it)

like this

no primary woodland left
collage from the Ramblers magazine

I'd never seen a Caledonian pine forest
a surprising find
Made from Tibetan yaks
as old as yew
long steep up
strenuous sixteen k
rare mosses, ferns
lead mining
lengths and difficulty within the glen
Corsican pine and larch
Sitka spruce
Notable roots,
to shout about

step to the past
round the edge of the tarn
by a spider's thread
no primary woodland left
either side of low tide
frosted landscape
wintry routes
the pack-horse trail continues
more loch than rock
steeply down
heather-high
to the far corner
boot control
in the hedgerows
foot crisis
soggy socks
mud-clad
fewer leaves on trees

                        awkward
            rich
                        prehistoric
                             the linear trail
                        land-hungry
                                    long mountain ramble
            star-lit winter's walk
                                         run of the mill
                favourite druid's berry
                                        trespass on moorland
        spiritually more on the hoof
                                        the joy of walking

                        to shout about

                                             right of way right

snug by the wall
the one the pennine wind forgot
Todmorden's first apricot

slmoat sing

crumble compost
add water
damp and press
adden more, no air
bubbles scatter leeks
seed generously over
earth scatter plastic
clumsily-holed
containers away

tongues wag
slittle nippets
of life chippings in

broad beans in plastic
shabby easily broken
 yet they cost the earth yet
they cost the earth they
soil cake-making
unless damp will fall
root trainers corrugated root
follow the line growing through
long and straight spread spread the earth
spread spread spread

sometimes planting forgotten we dig back
working together so well we slmoat sing

Joinings I
for Malc & Sue, October 2013

Shall I describe you as some other couple
who've come to plight their troth this sunny day
or are you something else, are you both double
that — mature and wise and brave enough to say

yes this is the person that I choose
to spend my life with: even though they see
my imperfections well, they don't refuse
but welcome them with love as part of me

yes — both say this happily, turning to look
straight in each other's eyes, with love, delight
reading their partner like a favourite book
with which, though earthbound, they can now take flight

to explore life's offers openly, together
and share with us in rain and sunny weather.

out of twelve hundred
kinds of English apple
you pluck me

Joinings II
for B & A, November 2013

nurtured by densities of heat, shade, rain
two sets of stems, leaves, scented petal heads
sprung glorious from unsuspecting flower beds
of varying soils, find ways up to the sun

but wait, before they meet, the first must oversee
witness of beginnings, the progress from their roots
cajoling, sheltering, of smaller shoots
sometimes with love, sometimes unwittingly

the other, youngest, last let loose
yearns to uncurl her shadowed leaves in sun
striving to catch her sisters who've begun
before her, singing colours spun of gold

this practised, now they stand in light of day
contrasts entwined in dazzling display

```
on                    ffo
        theeht
          vine
      sun dried yellow
   indoor baby peeled blush
 salad tomato grenadier skinned
red dwarf beef cherry juice tinned
 wild love apple puree ketchup
   ripe chopped plum alicante
    paste fried sliced green
     sauce chutney lycoper
      sicolycopersicum
```

Never caught

　train
　tops　trees
　grow ing　higher bank
dry black sticks　crow

man woman cat
　moving close　ground
undeterred　　　horizontal plane
　crows　nt stir
　　figures stop
call　possibility　shift
vertical　opens
　　fear
crow response　Lift
　air
　ground-hugging
figures move
Why
　tops　trees　railway
　part-way　hill

　days
　sun　low　rising
seed　　spread

sky-ward　hill-ward
　tree tops t　take
lifting　meadow hill
high　fly
　spy　　sycamore
　　glance
　low-roofed hut　pole

follow
perching upper branches
 lower bluetits
dotted   tree
       wait   order
checked   crows

sun shifts sky
 take
 taster crow
descends
 grab seed

alert feathered shapes
 movement   in
 red brick framed   glass   Opening
 hut   pole

   come
       shout
 never caught
     crows

W

on bor

v cold night
v cold night

got up twice to pee

I slept but cold kept waking me

first time behind caravan

meditation wrapped in fleece hat scarf sleeping bag and blanket but on floor
to put on fleece   felt useless
?? cant interact with anyone rigid unopened
got up to get blanket
made toast (with help)

ate

breakfast—managed to light stove and m'they are instantly friendly to each other

going up and cuddling'ake tea and find porridge pot bowl and cook it
washed up in stream—bits of porridge norom—hote to wash in fast flowing
water

folded large plastic ried stones weeded

watched / petted lambs one keeps butting my arm in hopes of
orphaned
milk   lambs from
different
mothers   2 minutes later anyway

I remember the
odd when I

58

behind cloud Swedish Finns watching the east at sunset seeming to see it as
look West
It's a soft pastel pale—more orange through perspex than
outside and the East is a deep soft blue
The sunset is late today,

Diary no
tes *from*   *gift-econ*
                    nomy veg
                                        an edible a
        gro-fores
                                                try
                            garde
    n project

anyway chaffinch

that anyway chaffinch
about branch +
perched wind

ff swinging to write
o   the time it took
in   in
swinging

Caravan sounds

loud

closer to weather.
   bird   softer and drumming
 rain   baas
                   on window and roof   baas
     rocking in wind   -
    of lamb   -
        twits   -
                         -   constant slight ripple
Pheasant wing flutter   -   kwaak
       twits   trilly and
           - - - -
                high,
         roar -   -
  Wind
  of water
    what might have been a nightingale
      -     -   -

        (5th)   Toaw Toaw
                               Flappflutter
       -    -
And pheasant
        More lamb
    and bird   wit   wit   wit
P   tu   tu   tu
        heasant wing   - - - - - -

                 faint
      trill   maa
                      The weather-topped hills

                    Windmill makes noise
                    sometimes like car / plane
                    engine – as if someone has turned it
              on   what night have
               and   then
                   has the wind I feel caused it to
             turn   or - - -   it is   a fan
                   (4th) causing wind to
                  - - - -
                       flow round me
                  twit twit twit twit

                     and many
                     more
                           Nut
                      h
                         atch?

as the sun drops

last hour or so before transplanting lettuce   pushing all the bracken, in a
watching   sunset starts   in space cleared   pull it down the side of the
sunset with   watering cans and rainbutts   I put another in a planter   racing to write before
thrush behind the   so does the temperature   to write before
in bursts   developing orange to vit peppers   light fades   strong red
slowly getting to grips with camp kitchen   doing its own half hour to toilets   clearing bed of wire and   east soft
thing   today replanting surviving garlic and pink N + S
        lamb maas onion closer together   flapping stream   nothing
        sheep baas my own caravan
I hear the roots tear   of hunger, of slightly battery tingle
                to deter mice from   onions seem to sit on the soil   every time it lands it
And yet digging them up to replant   sings or calls
chaffinch flying around
the trees fairly close   is that brook going to babble all night?   to nail to strut

watering – hard heavy

a good 8 feet

transplanted calabrese

Digging a patch before sowing seed and pulling out the raspberry
That's a cracker says

only I forgot to plant one
the whole bed
and pulling out stringy roots (like a long hair in a
sna
sometimes v long

and turning over clods
'The moment is the goal' I say at one point

like sankhara
ghetti sauce)

Budd

and we discuss, or rather he

I think (difficulties Vipassana)
and 4 kinds of lettuce

v satisfying to pull them out

his

å

up

m and enlightenment

that th

is suits our

action of

di

gg

ing

63

taken apart, the cabbage
becomes all heart
and leaves

memory
                                re wind and sun
            could be water
pheasant hot footing it past my caravan
                                , a gift from Nature
            on a mission
            computer — with all the wind there's lots of electricity
            unconcerned   aiming in the direction of
      wet windy weather just right for indoor work.
                  — away from where he is   fed
    behind
                        the spelt and rye
            past them   not use elect
                  needs 3rd   time
                  windless sunless winter
      the replanted lettuces
                  Oh wonderful
                        gobbling later

all hale heart never-
failing kale, hungry gap food
economy of scale

As I am adding notes to the
Some time before I realise there's a bird feeder just there
says I am conscious of sound of wings   the shadow
the shadow of a small bird on
of a
      twig on   CHAFFINCH   the opposing page, twig
eye, on birds on ground   just by the feeder[arrow   The chaffinch comes close
     to sketched outline] // and   here it is
flying past close above my head
on this page   Their patience   CHAFFINCH
  too
The twigs bend / move when the birds land on
As I am adding notes to the top of
They move away and send   Mine in watching them   and shadow with a
small bird on   the shadow of a   twig
on   the opposing page, twig   just   by the
feeder[arrow   to sketched outline] // and
here it is on this page
  too

              The patience of birds

Briefly waged vegan & instantly friendly lamb

opportunity to instil tenderness in one short life

   motherless lamb

a little window into the meat industry

   butting

fattening up

   , tight woollen curls

for slaughter

   the wiry wry feel of it

To return to pheasant for a moment

the completely contrasting colours and
either its vibrations or my red and black hat
feeding pheasants   a pattern

3 appeared; cock, 'hermaphrodite/inbetweener] hen
male coat looks like a kimono

PHEASANT

the colours
it has two little tufts on its head - like
said v unusual never did when stranger was

[sketches]

his feet/toes are spread on the ground but his lifts and closes them to walk lift in
The other two didnt
see holes in grass - voles?

says no slug problem as no cats. voles, pheasants, mice eat
them.
perhaps they think I'm a pheasant

when he walks

Writing on empty lines poem

give me press and I
will go anywhere windy
   it's so salacioius
pet pet, patronise
make me small
      it's the only way
oh kiss me, the irony
            of
   togetherness
never say we didn't
never to me my dog
my little piece of what
cry the birds   flying
above   calm, calm, calm
   cry the birds

and addiction

Nettle

also carrot

in the light
beautiful, green,

then gets up, stretches, and walks

nettles in carrots

with sting removed
away. "A cat sits until it is done sitting,
two top leaves
toothed
and then gets up, stretches, and walks wide
Tree News, spring-summer
David Nash:
Shaping the language of
about to go for
two grades of stings
away." A cat sits until it is done
on stalk
sitting, and then gets up, stretches, and
each point of jagged leaf
walks away. "A cat sits until it is done

sitting and fix (weeding them)
good for tea and greens

stop. feathery carrot leaves

I've been stung thru jersey / trousers **stop.** two grades of stings
thinning carrots
nettles lurking beneath **stop.** on stalk
on end of each point of jagged leaf
stop. like to weed / pull / tease out nettles more
separating herbs from **stop.** to replant herbs
carrots nettles growing

It has to be seen, has to be consummated, for it to become whole.

stop.

weeds nip in quick – that's what weeds wild carrot has no carroty
My fingers start to tingle **stop.** root
get up to go to polytunnel
stop.
Weeding nettles getting to know them
stop.
they sting you too **stop.**
carrots were purple
the Dutch bred them patriotic **stop.**
I like to pick nettles bare handed
st op.
compulsion to weed / thin both
st op.

delicate soft caring job,
, stung by nettles (I have none)

I looked at them Nettles
am a nettle

I too

they

sting

I respond

71

too many nettle stings.

By four they really are buzzing

rub them with basil?   cream? aloe juice?

a bit better -

gloves make me clumsy   V strong.

expecting them to   cream?

swell up.

so many nettles,

better not pick nettles bare-handed any   I mis-pick with

sifting through carrots with gloves   gloves   **But**

breaking off carrot strands,

Vague memory of nettle

but

ed some,   on hands.

They start to sting more

what might be dock leaf   And does writing bring it on?

On return

dock leaf!   pick one and rub   see

again. Was it not

their jaws/faces ready to crunch.   also prickly faintly marked with

blood? blotches no longer stinging

now my fingers are nettle-tingling again –

yourself is like Or sitting in the caravan? Or

Or nettle stings   off

Stimulates the   hands lightly for heart-attack the sting

on   **Trying to define**

red

and   I thought it wasnt   The stinging

stinging spots   with   returns

stinging   I see the feathery carrot leaves

warm I see the

when I put my mind to it   different

melody and track beneath   lively warm world as organic

but I could woke up incredibly   how we see

didnt come up as high as my

as much continuous with the physical

in my toes and   reverse

🍎 but I think

feathery carrot leaves and nettles beneath

–   **trying to bite your own teeth.**

one and then the other

how the two create something different

Am listening more intently and

choicely You and I are all

picking out under-melodies

🍎 maw (jaw)

continuous with the ocean, being working

Nettle   plants,

Connected with

everything , more

(like the nettles)

more intimate with

universe as a wave is

feeling

x warmer

its sweet yellow fleshy roots
snaffled up before
    you can say parsnip

Lovely horses

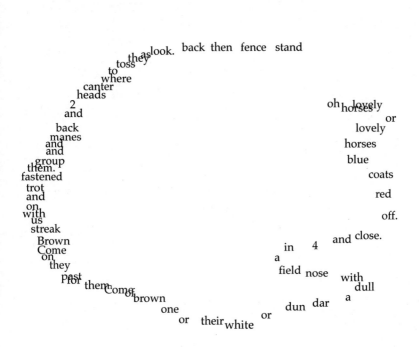

they look. back then fence stand
toss
to
where
canter
heads
2
and
back
manes
and
and
group
them.
fastened
trot
and
on,
with
us
streak
Brown
Come
on
they
Past them Come
brown
one
or their white or

oh horses lovely
or
lovely
horses
blue
coats
red
off.

and close.
in 4
a
field nose with
dull
a
dun dar

On walk to busstop
I'd been talking of
memory, elsewhere,
africa, getting on
a roll, memory,
elsewhere, africa,
memory, elsewhere
africa memory
elsewhere africa
memory elsewhere
africamemoryelse
whereafricamemory
elsewhereafricamem
oryelsewhereafrica
memoryelsewhere
Tsaysandit
tilts
me
off.

shall we
not

shall we not dig too deeply
into those earthy details of
what may promise optical
or otherwise benefits as
part of that mysterious
deal offered by mums
all over – carotene
that see-in-the-dark
xray power which
we have been told
has bedded down
is hidden in the
humble home-
grown carrot
that we have
all crunched
in the keen
desire to
gain its
powers
in health
intense
in taste
vibrant
shapely
rooted
in its
oran
gen
es
s
!

I n the field

remembered
horse outline
shifting he will not look

lunchtime I call him over, he
turns away
canters downfield

late night return
up hill
eyes on lighted window

sound, movement
warm saliva
breath whickering

what is he saying
repeated
carrotcarrotapplecarrotappleapplecarrotapplecarrot

the fiery raw rush
               of a rapid reddish

radish root

Crows feed first

most days at some point
when the sun is low or rising
over the hedge behind the sycamores
seed is spread —
place predictable, time not

minutes after there's no bird in sight
      droves fly in

bluetits congregate
picked out in line
on the laburnum tree
  a shadow
fly momentarily away:
up down off course
and flutter back
to wait and watch
as if by order

CROWS
FEED FIRST

waxwings

clattering the air
　　they swirl
　　air clattering
away from movement / presence
　　— cat, human
in a group — 33, 34
intent on the red-berried tree
strip it dry strip it high
　　I move up / away / up the bridge
and they
perched high together on a tree top
on the opposite high bank
　　of the railway
swirl down to the lower branches
for less than a minute
　　tabby behind me, camera-happy neighbour ahead
and then air-rattling
blast that cat
swirl up to the top branches
　waiting, no berries, safer, so stripped
and something disturbs them
up round clatter away
leaving the tree and the sky to
a couple of large black crows
　　and us. I'll have to get that cat in
　　　mutters the birdwatching
　　　　　　　　neighbour

off the hook

slumber my vegetable
love like the plant you
forgot to water
swell butternut rich

curve your body like flame
away from the sun-
dial that is pulling me,
scuttering.

chunky, nobbly-eyed
the potato says 'hi,
will you be my friend?'

outside the dark quiet of the attic

the hoot of an owl